D1435504

07600

Christian
faith and practice

The fish is a symbol of Christian faith.

Brian Knapp and Lisa Magloff

The Christian faith

One must believe in certain things with mind, heart and soul; and then live by them in the course of everyday life. Faith is always personal and individual. Each person follows the faith they choose. Here are some main parts of the Christian faith.

Christian beliefs

▶ God has three parts – the Father, the Son (Jesus Christ) and the Holy Spirit. God is the Creator of the universe through the Son and the Holy Spirit.

▶ All people are born with sin and may know salvation only through Jesus Christ, the Son of God.

▶ Jesus Christ was born of Mary, a virgin, was crucified on the cross, then resurrected from the dead and now sits at the right hand of God the Father.

▶ We are only on Earth for a single lifetime, but after death, we will be judged by God and will either achieve salvation and live forever with God in Heaven, or be forever denied the sight of God in Hell.

▶ The Holy Bible is sacred scripture and the only word of God.

▶ Goodness comes from our relationship with Jesus and with God the Creator.

▶ There is evil in the world, but it can be overcome.

How to be a Christian

Sin and unhappiness come from not following the will of God. Salvation comes from having faith in Jesus Christ and the message he taught. We must place all of our trust in God and Jesus Christ and accept the word of God as written in the Holy Bible. By repenting our sins, and living a life of virtue and obedience to God, we can become closer to God, but only God can grant us ultimate salvation.

Find out more

Look at the companion Curriculum Visions book, 'Christian church'.

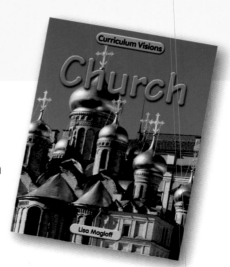

Contents

As you go through the book, look for words in **BOLD CAPITALS**. These words are defined in the glossary.

 ## Understanding others

Remember that other people's beliefs are important to them. You must always be considerate and understanding when studying about faith.

Objects used in Christian worship.

What it means to be Christian

Christianity is a belief in Jesus as God's presence on Earth in human form.

Christianity is the world's largest faith. About one in every three people in the world is brought up in the Christian faith.

A Christian is anyone who considers themselves to be a Christian, that is, anyone who believes in the life and teachings of **JESUS OF NAZARETH**, or **JESUS CHRIST**, the founder of Christianity.

Knowing God through Jesus

Jesus was born Jewish, and the word Jesus is the Greek form of the **HEBREW** name Yeshua, or Joshua. This was a common Jewish name in ancient times, it means 'the Lord is salvation'. The word Christ is the Greek form of the Hebrew word '**MESSIAH**', meaning '**ANOINTED**'.

Jesus said that knowing him is the doorway to a special relationship with God, so being a Christian is about finding your own special relationship with Jesus.

There are many ways of doing this, which is one reason there are many different kinds, or traditions, of worship within the Christian faith. You may be familiar with some of these traditions, such as **ORTHODOX**, **CATHOLIC**, **BAPTIST** and **ANGLICAN** traditions.

▲ Jesus said that knowing him is the doorway to a special relationship with God. This wooden door in Austria shows Jesus waiting to be let inside.

Another Christian tradition is called Evangelism. An Evangelical is someone who feels a special relationship with Jesus through having received his spirit in their lives, which is also called being 'born again'.

▲ These worshippers are thinking about what Jesus means to each of them.

▲ These children are learning about the life of Jesus in Sunday school.

All of these groups of Christians believe in Jesus, but they each have different ways of following his teachings.

Christianity

Christians believe that God revealed himself to mankind through his Son, Jesus Christ, and that Jesus' teachings are the teachings of God. To Christians, Jesus is a part of God, and not just a human **PROPHET** telling about God's works.

Being Christian is not just a matter of being born into a Christian family. Rather, it is a matter of faith. All through his life Jesus called for faith; faith in himself, in his teachings, in God, and in the **KINGDOM OF GOD**. Being a Christian is to have faith in these things.

A Christian not only accepts the major Christian beliefs, but also follows the way of life that Jesus taught, and is a part of the Christian community.

The Christian community

Through his teachings, Jesus explained that the most important thing is to love God. If someone has faith but not love, they have not achieved the Christian goal. Jesus taught that one way to love God is to love others as you love yourself.

Christians use the important word 'fellowship', which means life together as Christians, sharing with each other and supporting each other.

Jesus commanded his **DISCIPLES** to spread his message to the entire world by teaching people about Jesus and by doing good works. So, in addition to faith and prayer, a Christian life should involve helping others, **REPENTANCE** (page 19) and teaching others about Christian ideals.

A Christian way of life

There are many ways that Christians express their faith in everyday life.

Communal worship is at the heart of Christian faith and many Christians express their faith by going to worship in a church at least one day a week. But for many people, worship does not begin and end in church, and they may choose to express their faith in various ways every day.

Church worship

Church worship varies from one tradition to another. It may involve all sorts of activities. Reading from the Bible, confessing sins, singing hymns, songs and **PSALMS**, praying quietly and out loud, and listening to a **SERMON** may all be parts of church worship.

▼ Singing hymns, or songs of praise, is an important part of church worship services.

► Church worship may be led by a vicar or a priest.

In all churches, the main day for worship is Sunday. This is the Christian day of rest, or **SABBATH**. On Sunday, most churches have longer services than on other days of the week.

Church services may also change from one time of the year to the next. For example, at Christmas, children may put on a play, called a **NATIVITY PLAY**, which tells the story of Christmas. Or at Easter there may be a **PASSION PLAY**, which tells the story of Easter.

Everyday prayer

Many Christians also pray outside church. For example, they may say **GRACE** before meals, to thank God for the food they are about to eat. Others may say a prayer before going to bed, or at other times in the day. These are all ways of bringing God into everyday life and feeling closer to God.

Jesus told his followers to love their neighbours and give their wealth to the poor.

▶ Prayer can be done alone or with others.

Many Christians choose to follow these instructions by doing volunteer work, either individually or as part of an organisation, or by raising money for good causes.

Jesus also told his followers to spread the word of God, and so many Christians worship through teaching others about Jesus. These are Evangelists. Evangelists may teach in their own country, or they may go to another country to try and teach non-Christians about Jesus. Evangelists have also worked to translate the Bible into almost every language.

Monks and nuns

Some people choose to dedicate their entire lives to God. They may become clerics and minister to a church congregation, or they may live as monks or nuns.

Monks and nuns make solemn vows to God to live lives of poverty, chastity and obedience to God. In some traditions, they remain secluded in a **MONASTERY** and spend most of their time in prayer. In others, they live in the community and spend much of their time engaged in good works.

Some Christians choose to live for a short time in a monastery. This is called a retreat. During a retreat, almost everything you do focuses on worship and on God. This is another way for ordinary people to feel closer to God.

The life of Jesus

The life of Jesus is important because through it Christians find their faith.

The Stations of the Cross are a series of fourteen events from the sentencing of Jesus to death by Pontius Pilate to being placed in the tomb. They are a historical record of the events leading to the death of Jesus. In many churches, they are represented by pictures or plaques. These pictures are usually mounted on the walls inside a church.

The pictures are a way of visiting each of the sites of these events, which is what the early Christians were able to do. Prayers are normally said by people as they walk from one station to the next.

▲ Jesus is condemned to death.

▲ Jesus is made to carry the cross he will be crucified on to Calvary, the place of execution.

Christians follow the life and teachings of Jesus of Nazareth, or Jesus Christ. The story of Jesus' life is central to Christian faith.

The birth of Jesus

The **NEW TESTAMENT** in the Bible tells the story of Jesus' life.

Jesus was born in Bethlehem, Palestine (near modern day Israel) to a woman called Mary. Mary was later called the **VIRGIN MARY**, because Christians believe that Jesus was born through the will of God, not by having relations with her husband Joseph.

By tradition, Jesus' birth date is usually given as the year 0 in the **WESTERN CALENDAR**.

Jesus was born when the family had to make a trip from their home in Nazareth to Bethlehem in order to be counted in a **CENSUS**. There was no room at the local inn so the family had to sleep in a stable or barn. This is where Jesus was born.

Jesus the preacher

Jesus grew up in the Jewish faith. At that time, hereditary Jewish religious leaders were the only ones

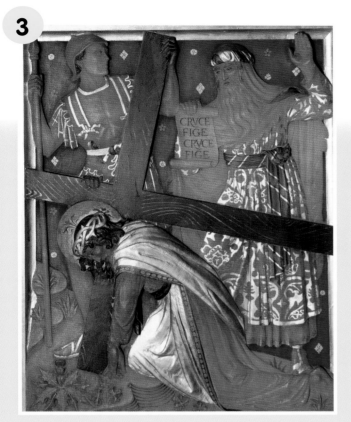

3

▲ Jesus falls the first time. He is pulled up and made to continue.

4

▲ He meets his mother, Mary, on the way.

5

▲ Simon of Cyrene is made to help Jesus carry the cross.

allowed to perform the most sacred worship services. But Jesus preached that anyone can pray and worship God in their own way. This made the religious leaders very angry.

Jesus preached that he was the Messiah and the way to God was through him. For example, Jesus forgave people their sins in the name of God, something that the Jewish religion taught would only happen when the **MESSIAH** arrived.

Jesus also performed miracles such as helping the blind to see, curing **LEPERS**, walking on water, and he even brought a dead man back to life.

A number of people began to believe that Jesus was speaking the word of God and they began to follow him.

His 12 closest and most loyal followers were called the **DISCIPLES**, or the **12 APOSTLES**.

Jesus is killed

Jesus was hated by the Jewish religious leaders because some people had begun calling Jesus the King of the Jews. This posed a threat to their power and they wanted him disposed of.

Weblink: www.CurriculumVisions.com

6

▲ Veronica, one of Jesus' followers, wipes Jesus' face.

7

▲ Jesus falls the second time.

8

▲ The women of Jerusalem weep over Jesus.

Palestine was at that time part of the Roman empire. The Jewish high priest took Jesus to the Roman governor of Palestine, Pontius Pilate, who condemned him to **CRUCIFIXION** (a Roman method of putting people to death by nailing them to a wooden cross). Jesus probably died on a Friday, in the spring. He was 33 years old.

This is the most solemn part of the Christian story, but it is also the most important – Christians believe that Jesus suffered and died so that all humankind could be granted eternal life with God. By dying, Jesus voluntarily took upon himself the sins of the world and made it possible for others to achieve **SALVATION**. This was his task as the **SAVIOUR**.

The resurrection

After his death, Jesus' body was placed in a tomb and guarded by Roman soldiers.

The Romans were afraid that the disciples would try to take the body away. But three days later, when some friends came back to the tomb, the clothing they had wrapped the body in was still there, but the body was gone.

What happened is a matter of faith. Some Christians believe that Jesus was brought back to life (resurrected) by God as a real person, others believe that his resurrection was much more like a spirit, which becomes clear to the followers who carry on his message.

However, all Christians believe that after his death and resurrection, Jesus joined God in heaven.

9

▲ Jesus falls the third time.

10

▲ He is stripped of his clothing.

11

▲ He is nailed to the cross.

12

◄ He dies on the cross.

13

◄ He is taken down from the cross.

14

► He is placed in the sepulchre (tomb).

Weblink: www.CurriculumVisions.com

Statements of faith

Christianity involves having a personal relationship with Jesus, so there are some differences in what Christians believe. But certain main beliefs are shared by almost all Christians.

The creed

In the early days of Christianity people had to state what they believed before they were admitted into the church. This statement is called a creed. The word creed comes from the Latin word *credo*, which means 'I believe'.

Today, different Christian traditions might use different creeds. But the one here, called the Apostle's Creed, is the most common and will help you to see the main points of Christian belief:

▲ The three ends of this cross stand for the Holy Trinity: the Father, the Son and the Holy Spirit.

> **I believe in God, the Father Almighty, Creator of Heaven and Earth.**

This part of the creed tells us that Christians believe in one God, who created the universe and all that is in it.

The idea of the HOLY TRINITY, one God who exists in three different ways, is one of the deepest parts of the Christian faith. In this part of the creed, the words "the Father" refer to the part of God that is the Almighty Creator of the universe and everything in it. This includes not only the things we can see, such as the Earth and everything on it, but also those things that we cannot see or know, such as HEAVEN and HELL.

The other two parts of God are the Son and the HOLY SPIRIT. God the Son is Jesus, the human part of God.

God the Holy Spirit is the part of God's power that we can see on Earth. For example, if a sick person prays to God and is healed, they might say that the Holy Spirit healed them. You cannot see the Holy Spirit, but you can see the results of the prayer (healing).

> **...and in Jesus Christ, His only Son our Lord...**

Jesus is a form of God on Earth. He was both a part of God and human at the same time. Because of this, Jesus has a special relationship with God that no one else can share. This is why the creed says that Jesus is God's only Son.

... who was conceived by the Holy Spirit, born of the Virgin Mary...

This part of the creed tells us that Mary was a VIRGIN. God created the miracle of Jesus' birth through the power of the Holy Spirit, there was no man involved.

...suffered under Pontius Pilate, was crucified, died and buried.

A central belief in the Christian faith is that Jesus died and rose again. That is why the creed includes the words "died and buried", to affirm the belief in Christ's death.

He descended to hell. On the third day he rose again from the dead, ascended to heaven, and sits at the right hand of God, the Father Almighty...

Jesus died, but he will also live forever with God. The word "sits", instead of "sat" means that Jesus is with God right now and always.

...from whence he shall come to judge the living and the dead.

Christians have faith that if they follow the teachings of Jesus and REPENT (feel bad for) their sins they will be rewarded after death with everlasting life in Heaven. The word "judge" in this part of the creed refers to the belief that after you die, God, through Jesus, will decide if you have repented.

I believe in the Holy Spirit...

The Holy Spirit is God's power on Earth, it is the bond that unites us with God.

...the holy catholic church...

The term "church" is used by Christians in different ways. It can mean a building in which Christians meet to worship. It can also mean a type of Christianity, such as the Roman Catholic Church, or the Eastern Orthodox Church. Or it can mean all of Jesus' followers, also called the worldwide fellowship of Christians. This last meaning is the one used here.

When the word catholic is spelled with a small 'c' it means 'everyone'. So, the words "holy catholic church" in this part of the creed means the entire worldwide Christian community.

...the communion of saints...

The term "communion of saints" means the coming together of all of Christ's followers, both living and dead.

...the forgiveness of sins...

This part of the creed shows that God is willing to forgive any sin, as long as the person who committed it truly repents.

...the resurrection of the body, and the life everlasting.

For a Christian, "life everlasting" does not mean living exactly the same way they live now, only forever. Life everlasting means living in God's grace and in God's presence forever.

The Christian Bible

Jesus wrote nothing down. He relied on the memory of his disciples and others that came after them to do this important job for him.

The Bible is the written record of what God wishes us to know. The word Bible means simply 'book', and the Bible is the most important book in the Christian faith. The Bible is also called the Holy Bible and the Holy Scriptures. The word scripture means 'writings'.

The history of the Bible

The Bible was not written by a single person, or even in a single lifetime. It was written over many hundreds of years and by many different people.

The Bible consists of 66 separate books which are divided into two main parts, called testaments. The word testament means 'agreement', and the two parts of the Bible can be thought of as agreements of faith between God and people.

The two main parts of the Bible are the **OLD TESTAMENT**, which contains the history and sacred writings of the Jewish people before the time of Jesus, and the **NEW TESTAMENT**, which tells the story of Jesus and the Christian faith.

The Old Testament is sacred to both Jews and Christians, while the New Testament is sacred to Christians alone.

The New Testament

Jesus did not write his teachings down. Instead, he spoke directly to his audience. This is called preaching, and you could call Jesus a wandering preacher, because he went from place to place preaching.

After Jesus' death, four of his disciples – Matthew, Mark, Luke and John – wrote down Jesus' teachings and the story of his life, so that they could be spread more easily. These writings are called the Gospels of Matthew, Mark, Luke and John and they are the main part of the New Testament.

▲ The earliest Bibles that we have copies of were written in Greek, like the Greek Orthodox Bible.

nce; make not my Father's house merchandise).

isciples remembered that it was al of thine house hath eaten me

swered the Jews and said unto n shewest thou unto us, seeing t these things?

wered and said unt mple, and in three da

the Jews, Forty and in building, and wilt days?

ke of the temple of his body. fore he was risen from the dead, embered that he had said this l they believed the scripture, which Jĕ'şŭs had said. n he was in Jĕ-rú'şă-lĕm at the feast day, many believed in they saw the miracles which

did not commit himself unto e knew all men,

13 And no man hath ascended up to heaven, but he that came down from heaven, *even* the Son of man which is in heaven.

14 ¶ And as Mō'şĕş lifted up the serpent in the wilderness, even so must the Son of man be lifted up:

15 That whosoever believeth in him should not perish, but have eternal life.

16 ¶ For God so loved the world, that he gave his only begotten Son, that whosoever believeth in him should not perish, but have everlasting life.

condemn the world; but that the world through him might be saved.

18 ¶ He that believeth on him is not condemned: but he that believeth not is condemned already, because he hath not believed in the name of the only begotten Son of God.

19 And this is the condemnation, that light is come into the world, and men loved darkness rather than light, because their deeds were evil.

20 For every one that doeth evil hateth the light, neither cometh to the light, lest his deeds should be reproved.

The word 'gospel' means 'good news' or 'glad tidings'. The Greek word for Gospel is 'evangelion', which is why some people who teach others about Christianity call themselves Evangelists, which means 'the bringers of good news'.

There are several other books in the New Testament. Most of these are concerned with the work of Jesus' followers, who carried on his mission after his death. This work is described in the book of **ACTS** and in the many Epistles (letters) written to the faithful by early leaders of the Christian church.

The purpose of Gospel stories

When Jesus preached, he often used stories to teach lessons about God, because stories are easily understood by ordinary people. We can all listen to a story and see how its meaning fits our lives.

The Gospels contain stories that Jesus told, and also the story of Jesus' life, death and resurrection.

▼ These children are reading a children's version of the Bible, which tells the stories simply.

The saints

Saints are people whose faith is so strong that God works through them on Earth. Saints are not found in the Bible, but have been named by churches over the centuries.

The word saint originally meant 'a true believer'. That is a person who, through having an unshakable faith, is seen as having an especially close connection with God. This strong faith allows God to work through them to accomplish something miraculous. This is why people often pray to the saints, so that the saint can act as a messenger to God.

Jesus did not speak of saints, but as the Christian church grew bigger, it began to celebrate the lives of people who had this special relationship with God.

▲ Saint George lived during the 4th century CE. This picture shows one of the stories told about him, that he killed a dragon.

▼ A worshipper shows her faith in the saints by kissing their picture.

▶ On the birthday or anniversary of a saint's death, worshippers may show the saint to the community by taking their statue in a procession from the church around the town. This celebration is in Disntis, Switzerland.

The importance of saints

Saints are an important part of Christian faith for many people. Many Christians go on **PILGRIMAGES** to places where the saints lived, or where some special event happened. In this way they hope to get closer to God so that they can be forgiven for sins, ask for help or give thanks to God.

Some of the earliest saints were people who were killed for their Christian beliefs. These people are also called **MARTYRS**. It is believed that martyrs are taken up into heaven directly by Jesus, so they are thought of as a kind of direct connection to God.

How saints are thought of

In some traditions, saints are respected and worshipped. This is especially important in Orthodox and Roman Catholic worship. The remains of saints (called relics) were gathered by people in past times and thought to have special powers.

Foremost among the saints are Mary, the mother of Jesus, and the 12 apostles. These saints are shared by all Christian traditions.

In many churches, there are statues and paintings of these, and other, saints which tell the story of their lives. Sometimes worshippers pray to the saints to help them.

There are hundreds of other saints. Some traditions have a process known as canonisation, in which someone is made a saint. After their death, a person can be nominated for sainthood. The person's life is examined closely to see if God worked through them to accomplish miracles or other great deeds.

Weblink: www.CurriculumVisions.com

The invisible world of God

Christians believe that there is an invisible world created by God and that they can be part of it by repenting their sins.

God created both the world that we can see and touch everyday, and an invisible world where God can be seen and known directly. This world, also called the **KINGDOM OF GOD**, can only be reached through God's grace.

The Christian name for God's invisible eternal kingdom is **HEAVEN**. Christians believe that if they have faith and follow the teachings of Jesus and repent their sins they will be rewarded after death with everlasting life in Heaven. If they do not do these things, they will have to live without the presence of God. The word for a place or way of being without God is **HELL**.

For some, Heaven is an actual place, a beautiful garden where God lives. For others, Heaven is not a place, but a state of being with God for ever.

Angels are messengers

Angels are the messengers between Heaven and Earth (the word angel means 'messenger'). Angels bring messages from God to people on Earth and provide spiritual guidance. No one knows what angels look like, but they are usually shown as looking like humans, but with wings. Some other names for angels are: archangels, principalities, powers, virtues, dominions, thrones, cherubim and seraphim.

Evil spirits

Just as there is evil on Earth, there is also evil in the spiritual world that God created. Those who do evil in the spiritual world are called demons and devils and live in Hell. SATAN (which means 'the enemy') is one name for the leader of these evil spirits.

For some, angels and devils really exist, while for others, angels and devils are the good and bad thoughts inside us. But either way, the angels work to bring people closer to God, while devils work to make people sin and take them further away from God.

Sin

To a Christian, a sin is an action that goes against the word of God. The first sin is in the Old Testament, when Adam and Eve eat the apple of the Tree of Knowledge, even though God has forbidden it. Adam and Eve put what they wanted before what God wanted – they thought of themselves before thinking of God. This is sin.

Forgiveness

In order to defeat sin and get closer to God, Christians must REPENT. That is, they must feel sorry for any sins they have committed. Sometimes this involves telling a priest or vicar about the sin, or doing PENANCE, which is an action or prayer that makes up for the sin. Other times it involves telling God, in a prayer, that you are sorry.

Feeling bad and saying sorry are not enough. In order to be forgiven by God, Christians must also regret what they have done and then reject it. They must start again, going in the other direction. One way to do this is to reaffirm a belief in Jesus.

Confirming your faith

For many Christians, it is not enough to be born into a Christian family. They must also make a commitment to accept the Christian faith in a ceremony.

The resurrection of Jesus Christ after his death is at the centre of Christian faith. So, when people make a commitment to accept Christian faith, they show that they accept the story of Jesus' life, death and resurrection through a ceremony called baptism. Baptism is a personal experience of the death and resurrection of Jesus.

During the baptism ceremony, a person is immersed or sprinkled with water. The water stands for being cleansed of sin. It also stands for dying and being resurrected by Jesus.

Being born again

Baptism is performed when a person enters the Christian community. Many people are baptised as babies. Because a baby cannot say what it believes, the parents and godparents make a commitment to Christianity on the baby's behalf. It is the godparents' duty to teach the child about Christian beliefs and practices as it grows up. Once the child has learned about Christianity, they can take part in a

▲ The baptism of Christ by John the Baptist.

ceremony called **CONFIRMATION**, which confirms their commitment to the Christian faith.

When Jesus began preaching, he first went through a baptism. Jesus was baptised by **JOHN THE BAPTIST** in the river Jordan. In this way, Jesus was showing that he had been reborn.

Today, some Christian traditions follow Jesus' example and go through the baptism ceremony as adults. In these traditions, the person being baptised first confesses their faith. They are then either sprinkled with water, or completely immersed in water. This symbolises being washed clean of sin and starting over, or being reborn in Jesus. This is sometimes called being 'born again'.

► In most Christian traditions, children are baptised when they are infants. At the baptism, they are given a godparent. This is the person who will be responsible for their religious education.

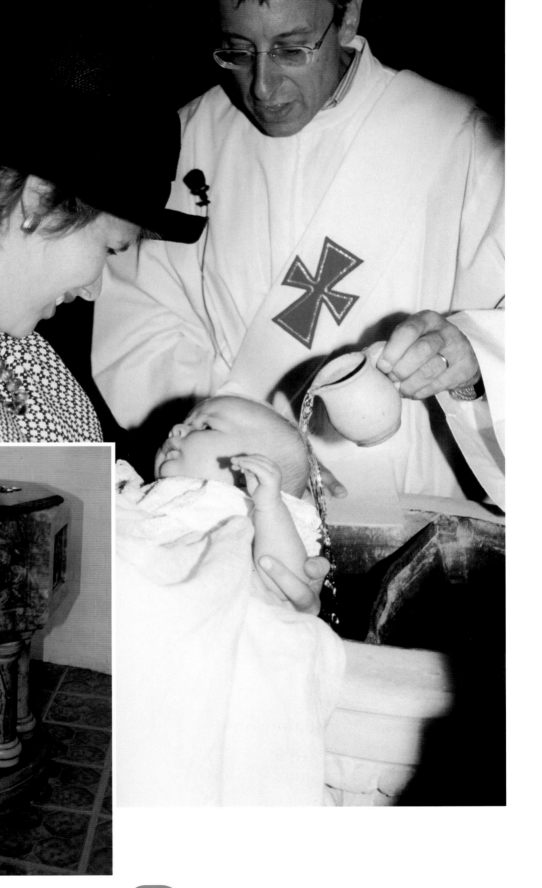

▼ The baptism ceremony takes place at a font, which contains water which has been specially blessed.

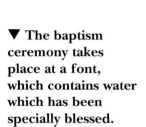

The heart of worship

Through the ceremony of Holy Communion, Christians share in Jesus' communion with God.

In most traditions, the heart of the Christian faith is a ceremony called **HOLY COMMUNION**, or **EUCHARIST**. The word Eucharist means 'thanksgiving'. Other names for this ceremony are Mass, Last Supper and Holy Liturgy.

Only people who have been baptised and who have publicly confirmed their faith can take part in this ceremony.

Holy Communion is a re-enactment of the **LAST SUPPER**. This was the last meal that Jesus ate with his disciples, on the night before he died. During this meal, Jesus handed his disciples bread and wine and told them that the bread was his body, and the wine was his blood. By eating the bread and drinking the wine, the disciples could share Jesus' contact, or communion, with God. Holy Communion is a way for all Christians to share the experiences of Jesus Christ.

◄▼ During the ceremony of Holy Communion, the priest or vicar blesses the wine and then gives each COMMUNICANT a sip of the wine.

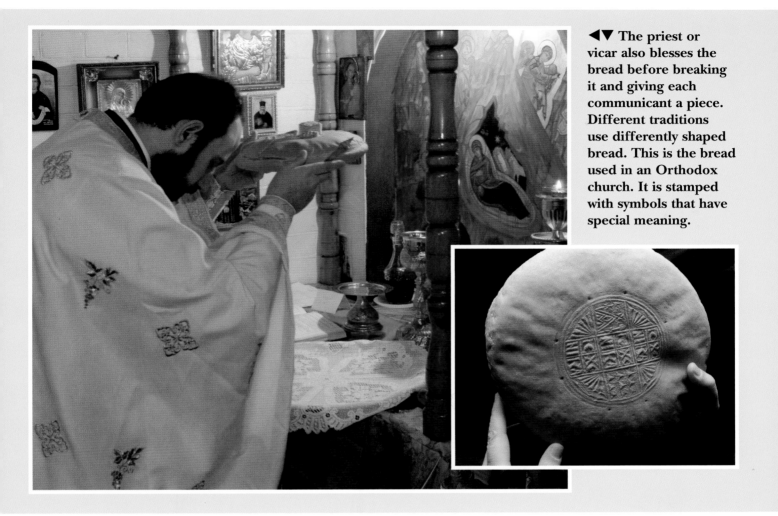

The priest or vicar also blesses the bread before breaking it and giving each communicant a piece. Different traditions use differently shaped bread. This is the bread used in an Orthodox church. It is stamped with symbols that have special meaning.

Different traditions and churches have different ways of performing the Holy Communion. For some, the bread and wine are reminders of Jesus' sacrifice. Others believe that Christ's body and blood are actually present in the bread and wine. But some parts are always the same.

The bread and wine always stand for the body and the blood of Christ. They are always given to all the members of the Church who have been baptised and confirmed.

▼ Here, a communicant is receiving a small piece of bread from a vicar. She will then eat the bread.

Using Christian symbols

There are many symbols used in Christianity designed to remind people about the word of God and the story of Jesus.

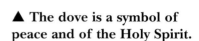

Symbols have been used in the Christian church since the earliest times for many reasons.

▲ The dove is a symbol of peace and of the Holy Spirit.

The earliest symbols

In the early days of Christianity, many Christians were persecuted and had to hide. Some symbols were used as a secret sign so the faithful could find each other. For example, the first letters of the words in the Greek phrase "Jesus Christ, Son of God, Saviour" form the Greek word ICHTHUS, which means 'fish'. A fish symbol was used by believers in the early days of persecution as a secret sign of their shared faith. One person would draw an arc in the sand, and the other would complete the sign to show his brotherhood in Christ.

Symbols that teach

Other symbols were used as a means of teaching Bible stories to people who were not able to read. For example, the dove is a symbol of the Holy Spirit.

It is taken from the story of Jesus' baptism, where the Holy Spirit appeared in the form of a dove.

Symbols are also used as a way of reminding believers of God's sovereignty over all creation. For example, the cedar tree stands for Christ. The soaring height to which this tree can grow is a reminder of the ideas of beauty and majesty. Because the cedar tree is an evergreen, and it is long-lived, it has also come to be associated with eternal life. For this reason, cedar trees are often planted in Christian cemeteries.

The cross

The most central symbol is the cross.

The cross symbol is a reminder of the crucifixion of Christ.

There are many shapes of cross. The empty cross is a reminder of the resurrection and the hope of eternal life. Another popular type of cross has the letters INRI above it (see pages 24 and 29). These letters stand for the Latin words *Iesus Nazarenus Rex Iudaeorum*, meaning Jesus of Nazareth, the King of the Jews. This is the inscription that Pilate ordered to be placed on Jesus' cross.

Some crosses have three buds or points on the end of each arm. These stand for the three parts of God – the Father, the Son and the Holy Spirit.

▲ The Christian fish symbol. Inside it are the Greek letters for ICHTHUS.

▲ When two candles are placed on an altar, they represent the way that Jesus was both human and divine.

Candles

Candles are another important symbol. The light of the candle calls to mind Jesus' words, "I am the Light of the World".

Worshippers light candles as a type of prayer. The light is a reminder of God's presence and of the light that Jesus brought into the world.

Other symbols

Some traditions use incense as the symbol of the rising of prayers, of spiritual sacrifice and of the sweet-smelling fragrance of the Kingdom of God. Flowers and fruit are signs of God's love, mercy and goodness.

▼ A censer is a container for burning incense used in worship. Just like the prayers rise up to present pleasing words to God, the incense drifts up to present God with a pleasing smell.

The Christmas festival

The Christian year is dominated by two major festivals. The first celebrates the birth of Jesus Christ.

▲ A nativity scene showing the baby Jesus, Mary, Joseph, three wise men and a shepherd.

The festival of Christmas, which celebrates the birth of Jesus Christ, is one of the most joyous festivals in the year.

The period of four weeks leading up to Christmas on December 25 is called **ADVENT**. This is a time of joyous anticipation (the word 'advent' means 'coming') as Christians prepare to celebrate Jesus' birth. Many of the Advent customs involve counting the days until Christmas begins.

The story of the nativity

During Christmas, the story of Jesus' birth, or the nativity, is told.

The story begins when Mary is visited by an angel from God who tells her that she will become pregnant and have a son. She asks the angel how this can happen as she is not yet married, but the angel tells her the child will be a child from God.

Mary was engaged to marry a carpenter named Joseph, and the angel also appeared to him and told him that he should marry Mary and name their child Jesus.

The trip to Bethlehem

Just before the baby was born, everyone had to return to their home village for a CENSUS. Joseph's home town was Bethlehem, in Gallilee, so Joseph and Mary went there, only to find that all of the inns were full of other people also returning for the census. The only space they could find was a stable. Here, Mary gave birth to Jesus.

The shepherds

Two other groups of people were also told about Jesus' birth. The first group were some shepherds who were out on the hillsides with their flocks of sheep. An angel appeared to them and said: "I bring you good news of great joy for everyone! The Saviour has been born tonight in Bethlehem! This is how you will find him: You will find a baby, lying in a manger, wrapped snugly in strips of cloth!" The shepherds ran to Bethlehem and found the baby Jesus, just as the angel said they would. This part of the story shows us that Jesus is the Lord of the poor and the humble.

The three wise men

Twelve days after Jesus was born, a group of educated and wealthy men from the East came to the stable. They had read an old story that a new star would foretell the coming of the MESSIAH. When they saw a new star in the sky, they followed it to Jerusalem and asked King Herod where they could find the newborn King of the Jews. King Herod asked the Jewish priests, and they told him that the baby Messiah could be found in Bethlehem.

When the wise men arrived in Bethlehem, the new star was shining directly overhead. The men gave Jesus gifts of gold, frankincense and myrrh. These were all symbols of kingship.

This part of the Christmas story shows that Jesus is also the Lord of the wealthy and the wise.

The celebration

On Christmas Night, Christians gather to celebrate Jesus' birth. This is traditionally done at midnight, although different traditions celebrate Christmas on different days. The celebrations last for 12 days. The last day of Christmas, January 6, is called EPIPHANY. This is the day the wise men came to visit the baby Jesus.

The Easter festival

The festival of Easter is at the heart of Christian beliefs because it marks the death and resurrection of Jesus.

▲ A cross used on Palm Sunday. It is made of palm leaves.

Easter Sunday is the most joyous day in the Christian year. This is the day on which Christ's resurrection is celebrated.

Easter is a remembrance of the day when Jesus was resurrected from the tomb in which he had been placed three days before. It is the oldest of Christian festival days.

Easter was originally called 'Pascha' after the Hebrew word meaning 'Passover'. (The Last Supper, Christ's death, and his resurrection all occurred during the Jewish festival of **PASSOVER**.)

Easter falls on the first Sunday following the first Full Moon on or after the first day of spring (March 21). But like other Christian festivals, Easter is not just one day, it is part of a cycle that begins long before Easter day itself.

Lent

The preparations for Easter take 40 days. This period is called **LENT** and it reminds Christians of the 40 days Jesus spent in the wilderness, being tempted by **SATAN**, following his baptism.

Lent begins with Ash Wednesday, when believers agree to make a personal sacrifice for the next 40 days. This reminds them of Christ's sacrifices in the desert. The days of Lent are spent in **REPENTANCE** and personal reflection.

▲ Jesus enters Jerusalem on a donkey as the people put palm leaves in front of him.

Holy Week

The last Sunday of Lent is Palm Sunday, when Christ's triumphal entry into Jerusalem is commemorated. Churches may be decorated with palm leaves, as a reminder of the palm branches that were strewn before Jesus as he rode into the city on the back of a donkey.

Palm Sunday is the beginning of Holy Week, which is spent thinking about the events of Jesus' last week before his crucifixion.

Thursday of Holy Week is called Maundy Thursday. Maundy Thursday is a commemoration of the Last Supper.

Friday of Holy Week is called Good Friday. Good Friday is the day of Jesus' crucifixion. It is a sombre day of reflection and repentance.

Easter Sunday

Easter Sunday is a day of joy and celebration at the resurrection. Early Christians were always baptised on Easter Sunday because of its deep significance for them. So there is a close connection between baptism – being brought into the church – and the resurrection.

During Easter, Christians believe that they pass through death and into a new life in Jesus Christ, just as Jesus passed through death and after three days rose from the dead to join God.

◄ Pictures of Jesus on the cross are used during Easter to help tell the story of Jesus' death.

29

Glossary

12 APOSTLES The 12 men who were chosen by Jesus to be his original disciples and to carry on his work after his death.

ACTS A book in the Bible which tells the history of the apostles after Jesus' death and the history of the early Christian church.

ADVENT A word which means 'coming', or the arrival of something that has been waited for, such as the coming of the Messiah. It is the period of four weeks which lead up to Christmas.

ANGLICAN A Christian tradition which began in England and is also called the Church of England.

ANOINTED To smear with oil. It was an ancient practice to rub kings and statues of kings with good-smelling oil as a sign of their power. The word anoint also means to recognise the right of someone to be king. For example, Jesus was anointed king by his followers.

BAPTIST A Christian tradition in which people are baptised as adults, usually by being completely immersed in water.

CATHOLIC A Christian tradition. The head of the Catholic church is the Pope in Rome. Catholicism was an early tradition of Christianity and was the only form of Christianity in Europe until the Middle Ages.

CE This abbreviation stands for 'common era'. This is another way of writing AD (which is a translation of the Latin words *anno domini*, or 'after the death of our Lord') when writing dates.

CENSUS A counting of all the people in a certain country or place. Census' are an important way for leaders to find out how many people are living in their country so they can plan how to tax them and care for them.

COMMUNICANT A person who takes Holy Communion.

CONFIRMATION A ceremony in some Christian traditions where people who were baptised as babies confirm their faith as young adults.

CRUCIFIXION A way that the ancient Romans used to kill criminals by nailing or tying them to a cross.

DISCIPLE A follower. This word is usually used to describe a close follower of a religious leader, such as Jesus.

EPIPHANY Also called the twelfth day of Christmas. This celebrates the day, 12 days after Jesus was born, when the wise men showed up in Bethlehem to proclaim Jesus as the Messiah.

EUCHARIST Another word for Holy Communion, the worship ritual where worshippers share bread and wine in remembrance of Jesus' last supper with his disciples.

GRACE Meaning kindness or the mercy of God. This also refers to a short prayer said before or after meals.

HEAVEN A place that was created by God and that is in the presence of God.

HEBREW The language spoken by the ancient Jews, in modern Israel, and in Jewish worship. At Jesus' time, most Jews spoke Aramaic, and used Hebrew for worship.

HELL A place that was created by God but where God is not present.

HOLY COMMUNION A worship ritual where worshippers share bread and wine as a reminder of Jesus' Last Supper with his disciples.

HOLY SPIRIT The part of God that we can see on Earth. But we cannot actually see the Holy Spirit, only the consequences of the actions of the Holy Spirit, when God decides to do something on Earth, he sends the part of him called the Holy Spirit to make it happen.

HOLY TRINITY Trinity means 'three' and the three parts of the Holy Trinity are God the Father (God in heaven), God the Son (Jesus), and God the Holy Spirit. The Holy Trinity is also the idea that God is one being with three different parts.

JESUS CHRIST The Son of God and the Messiah. The part of God that lived on Earth. The word Christ comes from the Greek word *christo* meaning 'anointed one'.

JESUS OF NAZARETH Another name for Jesus Christ. Jesus lived in Nazareth as a child. By the tradition of the time, most people only had a first name, so the place where they were born was added to their name to distinguish them from other people with the same name.

JOHN THE BAPTIST A preacher and prophet who lived at the same time as Jesus. John began the practice of baptising people as a way to prepare them for the coming of the Messiah.

KINGDOM OF GOD The idea that God will come to Earth and destroy all evil and save all of mankind, creating heaven on Earth.

LAST SUPPER The last meal that Jesus ate with his disciples. It was a Passover meal.

LENT A period of 40 days before Easter when worshippers give up something, such as sweets, in remembrance of the sacrifice that Jesus made.

LEPER A person with the disease of leprosy. Leprosy is a disease of the nervous system which causes the person to lose all feeling in their appendages. Eventually, parts of the body rot and may fall off. A cure has been found in modern times.

MARTYR A person who dies for their beliefs. Many early Christians were killed, or martyred, when they refused to give up their beliefs.

MESSIAH The person told about in the Bible who will save the Jewish people. Christians believe Jesus was the Messiah and that he came to save all people.

MONASTERY A large building or group of buildings where monks and nuns live.

NATIVITY PLAY A play or show which tells the story of Jesus' birth. Nativity means 'to be born'.

NEW TESTAMENT The part of the Bible that tells the story of Jesus and the apostles.

OLD TESTAMENT The part of the Bible that tells the history of the Jewish people from the beginning of time until before Jesus was born.

ORTHODOX A Christian tradition which is practised in many countries such as Russia and Ethiopia. It is the oldest Christian tradition.

PASSION PLAY A play which tells the story of Easter. This is also called the Passion of Christ. When used this way, the word passion means 'suffering'. So, a passion play tells the story of Christ's suffering on the cross.

PASSOVER The Jewish festival that commemorates the deliverance of the Jews from slavery in Egypt by God. It is celebrated with a special meal.

PENANCE To make up for doing something bad.

PILGRIMAGE A trip to a place that has religious importance, such as Jerusalem, or the site where a saint died.

PROPHET A person who has a special relationship with God. Through this relationship, God tells the prophet about what will happen in the future. To prophecy means to see the future.

PSALMS Poems in praise of God in the Old Testament that were sung or chanted as part of ancient Jewish worship and are also used today as part of both Jewish and Christian worship. Many Psalms have been turned into hymns.

REPENT/REPENTANCE To feel sorry for doing something bad.

SABBATH Another word for a day of worship. Sunday is the Christian Sabbath.

SALVATION The idea that every person can live forever in Heaven with God if they accept the Christian faith and beliefs.

SATAN The ruler of Hell. Christian tradition teaches that Satan was an angel who refused to obey God and as a punishment he was banished from God's sight forever. Christian tradition also teaches that Satan tries to get people to commit sins.

SAVIOUR Another way of describing Jesus. A saviour is someone who rescues or 'saves' another person. Christians believe that Jesus was sent to save people from their sins, so he is called 'the Saviour'.

SERMON A talk on a religious subject. In church, the vicar or priest may give a sermon during worship services. Jesus gave many sermons.

VIRGIN A person who has never had sex.

VIRGIN MARY The mother of Jesus Christ.

WESTERN CALENDAR The calendar that we use. There are different calendars, and some Christian traditions use an older calendar called the eastern calendar to calculate the dates of Christian holidays.

Index

Curriculum Visions

Curriculum Visions is a registered trademark of Atlantic Europe Publishing Company Ltd.

Atlantic Europe Publishing

Dedicated Web Site
There's more about other great Curriculum Visions packs and a wealth of supporting information available at our dedicated web site:

www.CurriculumVisions.com

First published in 2005 by
Atlantic Europe Publishing Company Ltd
Copyright © 2005
Atlantic Europe Publishing Company Ltd

Authors
Brian Knapp, BSc, PhD, and Lisa Magloff, MA

Religious Adviser
Aella Gage

Art Director
Duncan McCrae, BSc

Senior Designer
Adele Humphries, BA

Acknowledgements
The publishers would like to thank the following for their help and advice:
St James Church, Muswell Hill, London; St John the Baptist Church, Wightman Road, London; Father George Christidis of St Nictarios, Battersea, London; Rector Father Terence Phipps of St James Church, Spanish Place, London.

Photographs
The Earthscape Editions photolibrary, except page 15 (top) and 18 *ShutterStock*, and page 21 (main picture) courtesy *Mark, Katharine, Olivia and Lucy Dawson.*

Illustrations
David Woodroffe

Designed and produced by
Earthscape Editions

Printed in China by
WKT Company Ltd

Christian faith and practice
– Curriculum Visions
A CIP record for this book is available from the British Library

Paperback ISBN 1 86214 462 1
Hardback ISBN 1 86214 463 X

This product is manufactured from sustainable managed forests. For every tree cut down at least one more is planted.